NOAH'S ARK

NOAH'S ARK

Illuminated by
·ISABELLE · BRENT·

LITTLE, BROWN AND COMPANY
BOSTON   TORONTO   LONDON

This is the story of Noah.
Noah was a righteous man,
the one blameless man of
his time. He had three sons:
Shem, Ham, and Japheth.
God saw that the world
was corrupt and said to Noah, "I am going to
bring the whole human race to an end, for
because of them the earth is full of violence.

"Make yourself an ark with ribs of cypress; cover it with reeds and coat it inside and out with pitch. This is to be its design: you are to make a roof for the ark; put a door in the side of the ark, and build three decks, lower, middle, and upper. You will go into the ark, you with your sons, your wife, and your sons' wives. You are to bring living creatures of every kind into the ark to keep them alive with you, two of every kind of bird, beast, and creeping thing."

The Lord said to Noah, "Go into the ark, you and all your household. For in seven days' time I am going to send rain on the earth for forty days and forty nights, and I shall wipe off the face of the earth every living creature I have made." So to escape the flood Noah went into the ark. And to him on board the ark went one pair of all beasts, of birds, and of everything that creeps on the ground, two by two.

Wild animals of every kind, cattle of every kind, every kind of thing that creeps on the ground, and winged birds of every kind – all living creatures came two by two to Noah in the ark. They came in as God had commanded Noah, and the Lord closed the door on him.

At the end of seven days the water of the flood came over the earth. The flood continued on the earth for forty days. The ark floated on the surface of the swollen waters as they increased over the earth. They increased more and more until they covered all the high mountains everywhere under heaven. Every living thing that moved on earth perished, and only Noah and those who were with him in the ark survived.

When the water had
increased over the earth
for a hundred and fifty
days, God took thought
for Noah and the beasts
and cattle with him in the
ark, and he caused a wind to blow over the earth,
so that the water began to subside. The springs of
the deep and the windows of the heavens were
stopped up, the downpour from the skies was
checked. Gradually the water receded from the
earth, and by the end of a hundred and fifty days
it had abated. On the seventeenth day of the
seventh month the ark grounded on the
mountains of Ararat. The water continued to
abate until the tenth month, and on the first day
of the tenth month the tops of the mountains
could be seen.

Noah opened the hatch that he had made in the ark, and sent out a raven; it continued flying to and fro until the water on the earth had dried up. Then Noah sent out a dove to see whether the water on the earth had subsided. But the dove found no place where she could settle because all the earth was under water, and so she came back to him in the ark. He waited seven days more and again sent out the dove from the ark. She came back to him towards evening with a freshly plucked olive leaf in her beak. Noah knew then that the water had subsided from the earth's surface. He waited yet another seven days and, when he sent out the dove, she did not come back.

By the twenty-seventh day of the second month the earth was dry, and God spoke to Noah. "Come out of the ark together with your wife, your sons, and their wives," he said. "Bring out every living creature that is with you, live things of every kind, birds, beasts, and creeping things, and let them spread over the earth and be fruitful and increase on it." So Noah came out with his sons, his wife, and his sons' wives, and all the animals, creeping things, and birds; everything that moves on the ground came out of the ark.

God blessed Noah and his sons; he said to them, "Be fruitful and increase in numbers, and fill the earth. I am now establishing my covenant with you and with your descendants after you, and with every living creature that is with you, all birds and cattle, all the animals with you on earth, all that have come out of the ark: never again will all living creatures be destroyed by the waters of a flood, never again will there be a flood to lay waste the earth."

God said, "My bow I set in the clouds to be a sign of the covenant between myself and the earth. When I bring clouds over the earth, the rainbow will appear in the clouds. Whenever the bow appears in the cloud, I shall see it and remember the everlasting covenant between God and living creatures of every kind on earth."

The sons of Noah who came out of the ark were Shem, Ham, and Japheth; Ham was the father of Canaan. These three were the sons of Noah, and their descendants spread over the whole earth.

Illustrations copyright © 1992 by Isabelle Brent

All rights reserved. No part of this book may be
reproduced in any form or by any electronic or mechanical means,
including information storage and retrieval systems,
without permission in writing from the publisher, except by
a reviewer who may quote brief passages in a review.

First U.S. Edition

First published in Great Britain by Pavilion Books Limited

Extracts from Revised English Bible © 1989. Used by permission of
Oxford and Cambridge University Presses.

ISBN 0-316-10837-5
Library of Congress Catalog Card Number 91-35673
Library of Congress Cataloging-in-Publication information is available.

10 9 8 7 6 5 4 3 2 1

Designed by Elizabeth Ayer

Printed in Belgium by Proost

DATE DUE